The American Revolution

1764-1784

Patriotic history is frequently bad history. It has taught us an uncomplicated and prejudiced view of the American Revolution that it was a simple crusade by brilliant generals, brave soldiers, and a citizenry united by an undying spirit against a tyrannical and unbalanced king thousands of miles away. For those who wish to know, this book will teach us better.

To say that the American Revolution was merely a significant movement in modern history misses the mark and sells our founding fathers short. Not only did it lay the foundation for the United States, it gave unparalleled inspiration, guidance, and hope to hundreds of similar movements for independence for more than 200 years. Those who will best understand the Revolution are those who will take time to look deeply into the lives of those who sought freedom and liberty, the homes in which they lived, and the battlefields on which they fought. This book is an illustrated survey of those people, places, and times.

Benjamin Franklin's cartoon which appeared first In his Pennsylvania Gazette, 1754.

Warning inspired by the Stamp Act, from the Pennsylvania Journal, 1765.

The reconstructed Virginian capitol at Williamsburg. (Top Right)

George III, after an engraving by Thomas Frye. (above)

◀ Old South Meeting House, where many of Boston's early protest meetings were held.

The British troops landing in Boston, 1768. ▶

> "Military power... will never awe a sensible American tamely to surrender his liberty." — SAMUEL ADAMS, 1768

1763-1773

The nation that was to declare its independence from Great Britain in 1776 was hardly a nation at all but a string of separate colonies stretching from Maine (then a part of the Massachusetts Bay Colony) to Georgia—all separately governed in one form or another, their laws and religions were as different as their economics and social structure as unlikely a national beginning in history. Strangely enough, however, the strongest bond between them was their common allegiance to the King of England. By 1763 and the end of the French and Indian War, the colonists were well on their way to becoming Americans—they had been here for 150 years and had virtually governed themselves with little British interference. Still they held to the English common law and until political extremists portrayed George III as a miserable tyrant, the common man swayed little from his loyalty. Indeed, until the Declaration of Independence, July 4, 1776, George Washington and his officers of the Continental Army toasted the health of "their King."

Following the war with France, however, British attention was focused solely on the colonies. The national debt had doubled and economically Great Britain was in a serious depression. Parliament determined that the colonies should share the expenses of the Empire. This came in a long series of taxes and restrictions that affected nearly every phase of commerce. But one out of every five Englishmen was an American colonial without any seat in Parliament and the whole idea of taxation without any representation was a shock of mammoth proportions. The allegiance slowly began to crumble.

The Stamp Act, a tax stamp on legal documents, newspapers, contracts, and almost every piece of commercial paper, was the first internal tax Britain had ever imposed and it united the colonists in a

A propaganda depiction of the Boston Massacre, March 5, 1770, engraved by Paul Revere.

fury, from Boston to Williamsburg. Within a year Parliament repealed the Stamp Act but the peace was only temporary. Soon came other taxes on the importation of glass, paper, dyes, and tea. Though all but the tea tax were later repealed, the fires of revolt had been kindled. Urged on by Samuel Adams, political agitator and radical patriot, several colonial assemblies adopted nonimportation and nonconsumption agreements, serving notice on the mother country that the issue of rights and freedom was at stake and that regardless of economic impact, the colonies would stand firm in their determination to oppose these repressive legislations.

The Boston Tea Party

Then on a cold March night in 1770 violence erupted in Boston. Under the deft guidance of Sam Adams a band of ruffians assailed a small group of British soldiers with insults and snowballs. The soldiers fired into the mob killing five and wounding six. While a general calm prevailed for the next few years, the Boston Massacre was the catalyst Adams had sought. What had once concerned the wealthy merchants now concerned the common man. Committees of Correspondence were organized throughout Massachusetts and in June 1772 the British revenue cutter H.M.S. Gaspee was burned off Rhode Island.

Though the mechanics for rebellion were being created, the radicals remained in a minority. There was strong opposition to a break with England. Then the Tea Act was passed and again Adams had a victory. What he had been trying to do for so long was virtually accomplished overnight. Parliament authorized

the influential East India Company to ship tea to the colonies without paying import duties. Colonial opinion was united and within weeks the issue was brought to a head. This time the radicals, calling themselves patriots and dressing as Indians boarded three East India ships in Boston harbor on the night of December 16, 1773, and dumped 342 cases of tea into the sea. This was the "Boston Tea Party."

Tax on tea stirred up the Boston Tea Party. Townsmen disguised as Indians dumped cases of taxable tea into the Boston Harbor. (Top Right)
Burning of the British revenue cutter Gaspee, June 9,1772. Painting by C.D.W. Brownell. (Above)
Beaver II, an authentic replica of one of the three British ships involved in the Boston Tea Party, sails into Boston Harbor where it is exhibited at the Congress Street Bridge. (Right)

The First Continental

From 1772 to 1774 the American colonies began moving toward some form of intercolonial cooperation. As the events of '73 rapidly pushed public opinion toward unification, John Hancock proposed a general congress of all colonies. No sooner had he done so than Parliament closed the Boston port as a result of the "tea party." This punitive measure prohibited the loading and unloading of ships except for food and fuel shipped locally. The colonies were collectively infuriated. The Virginia House of Burgesses called for a day of fasting. Immediately the royal governor dissolved the

Charles Carroll of Carrollton, Maryland member of the Continental Congress and signer of the Declaration of Independence. Portrait by Thomas Sully.

assembly. Meeting unofficially, however, on May 27, the Virginia delegates declared "that an attack made on one of our sister colonies is an attack made on all British America and threatens ruin to the rights of all." It went even further and called for the colonies to meet in congress "at such place annually, as should be convenient to direct from time to time the measures required by the general interest." The foundation was laid. The First Continental Congress convened in Carpenters' Hall in Philadelphia on September 5, 1774. Some of the names that met that day—Silas Deane, Connecticut; John Adams, Massachusetts; Samuel Chase, Maryland; John Sullivan, New Hampshire; Stephen Hopkins, Rhode Island, and Peyton Randolph, Virginia.

Congress 1774

John Hancock, wealthy colonial merchant and member of the Continental Congress 1775-80. ▲

First Continental Congress
September 5, 1774 – October 6, 1774
Philadelphia.

Second Continental Congress
May 10, 1775 – March 2, 1781
Philadelphia, Baltimore, Philadelphia, Lancaster, York, Philadelphia.

Congress fled Philadelphia twice, December 12, 1776 and September 19, 1777 due to the threat of the British army.

The United States in Congress Assembled
March 3, 1781 – March 2, 1789
Princeton, Annapolis, Trenton, New York City.

First United States Congress
March 4, 1789 – November 17, 1800
New York City, Washington, D.C.

The First Continental Congress convened in 1774 in Carpenters' Hall, Philadelphia. ◄

While these great minds pondered over a "Declaration of Rights" and wrote letters to the King and to the Parliament, the public continued their protests to the Tea Act. On October 19, 1774, merchant Anthony Stewart of Annapolis, Maryland, set fire to his own ship, the Peggy Stewart, to pacify a lynch mob accusing him of having imported 17 packages of tea. While cooler heads continued to avoid armed rebellion, "tea parties" and other acts of protest occurred in villages and cities from Fredericktown, Maryland to Edenton, North Carolina. Opposition to the Crown was spreading through the colonies at a feverish pitch.

▲ Arthur Middleton, South Carolina member of the Continental Congress and signer of the Declaration of Independence. Portrait by Philip Wharton, after West.

◄ Anthony Stewart sets fire to the Peggy Stewart on October 10, 1774 in this painting of Maryland's Tea Party by Frank B. Mayor.

1775

It was no secret to Gen. Thomas Gage, commander of British troops in Boston, that the Americans were militarily active. The redcoats often stood by and watched the militia drill. What Gage did not recognize was the cold determination with which the colonists intended to resist British force. At no time was it more evident than the spring of 1775 when Capt. John Parker's men stood in formation across the Lexington Green in open defiance to the Crown.

On April 15, 1775, it was learned that Gage intended to send 700 troops on an unknown mission. Correctly assuming that the British had learned of the Patriot's storehouse of arms and ammunition at Concord, a "committee of safety" sent out word to move

Patrick Henry angers his fellow legislators as he protests the Stamp Act in the House of Burgesses. Painting by Peter Rothermel.

"I know not what course others may take, but as for me, give me liberty or give me death!"
—PATRICK HENRY, MARCH 1775

Faneuil Hall, Boston, has been called the "Cradle of Liberty" because of a speech delivered there in 1763 by James Otis, an early "apostle of freedom." The building (1742) is still used for public meetings and as a market place.

COLOR PHOTO: FRED JELLISON, JR.

William Dawes, the other man who rode with Revere to warn the people of Lexington. Painting by Gallagher. ◄

It was from the tower of Old North Church™, Boston, that on the night of April 18, 1775, two lanterns signaled the river route of British troops on their march to Concord. Services are still held each Sunday. ◄

"The Midnight Ride of Paul Revere," as depicted by W. R. Leigh. ▶

The Paul Revere House, the oldest frame building in Boston, and the site from which the famous rider started his journey April 18, 1775. ▼

the supplies. On the night of April 18 the alarm sounded—British troops were being ferried across the Charles River for the march on Concord. On prearranged lantern signals from Old North Church™ ("one if by land, two if by sea"), Paul Revere and William Dawes rode through the night warning of the approaching troops. By the time the column of British regulars, under Lt. Col. Francis Smith and Maj. John Pitcairn, reached Lexington, about 70 local citizens had assembled with arms.

Sensing the hopelessness of the odds, Parker ordered his men to disperse. They slowly drifted away. Then "the shot heard 'round the world" was fired, by whom no one will ever know. Pitcairn reported he gave no such order; the Americans denied it came from their ranks. But when the brief skirmish was over eight Americans were dead and two lay wounded. The day was not over. The Patriot fire was so heavy at Concord that Pitcairn withdrew and headed back to Boston.

What started as an orderly retreat, however, turned into a rout. From every stonewall, every tree, every house along the way, the colonials fired at the British. Every town along the way bristled with angry militia. Pitcairn limped into Boston with 73 dead and 174 wounded. The Americans suffered 49 dead and 41 wounded. But casualty figures meant little—it was a memorable day in history. The Americans had openly challenged the Crown. Nothing would ever be the same again on the North American continent.

Lexington and Concord set the stage for the years to come. Within days Boston was land-locked by 17,000 rebel troops and the British were in a state of siege. Things began happening rapidly. Fort Ticonderoga on the southern tip of Lake Champlain was captured by Ethan Allen and the Green Mountain Boys. Patrick Henry thundered in the Virginia Legislature, "Give me liberty or give me death." And on June 15, 1775, George Washington was unanimously elected by the Congress to command the Continental Army.

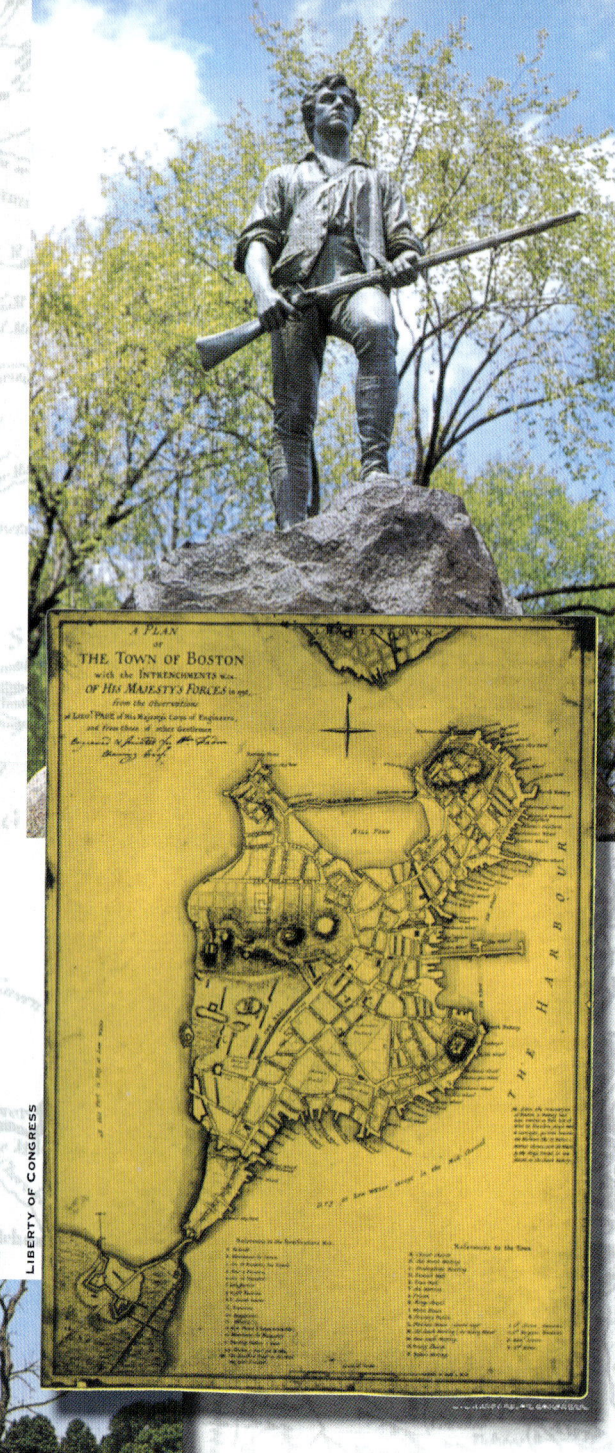

Town Plan of Boston, 1775. ▲

Henry H. Kitson's statue of the Minuteman stands on the Green at Lexington facing the direction from which British troops approached on the morning of April 19, 1775. (Top)

A reconstruction of the famous North Bridge at Concord, a part of Minuteman National Historical Park. ◀

"Stand your ground. Don't fire unless fired upon, but if they mean to have a war let it begin here"
— CAPTAIN JOHN PARKER, 1775

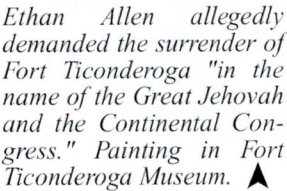

Ethan Allen allegedly demanded the surrender of Fort Ticonderoga "in the name of the Great Jehovah and the Continental Congress." Painting in Fort Ticonderoga Museum. ▲

General Sir William Howe, commander of British troops in America, 1775-78. ▶

Reconstruction of a British used blockhouse on Mount Hope overlooking Fort Ticonderoga. (Top Right)

Fort Ticonderoga, strategically located on Lake Champlain, played important roles in both the French and Indian War and the American Revolution. ▼

Before Washington could reach the Army at Cambridge, the first major battle of the Revolution erupted at Charlestown around a little hill on farmer Breed's property. Concerned with British defense plans, American forces under Gen. Artemas Ward took positions on first Bunker Hill and then Breed's Hill on the night of June 16. The next morning Gen. Gage ordered a direct frontal attack under Gen. Sir William Howe with 2,400 men. Waiting until they could see the "whites of their eyes," the Americans delivered a devastating fire, reeling the British back twice. A third attack succeeded, however, and the Americans were swept from the hill. It was a costly British victory. Howe suffered 1,100 casualties; the Americans 400. There was little for the Patriots to

The Battle of Bunker Hill

"Don't Fire 'til you see the whites of their eyes."
— BATTLE OF BUNKER HILL, 1775

be proud of, but the Battle of Bunker Hill, as it is mistakenly called, had a marked effect on the British. It was nearly a year before they again took the offensive.

While Washington tried to bring some order to the Continental Army, Congress became concerned about the British in Canada. Fearing that the St. Lawrence River and Lake Champlain would be used as an invasion route to the Hudson River, thus dividing the colonies, Congress ordered an American initiative using Fort Ticonderoga and Crown Point as a base for taking St. Johns and Montreal. St. Johns fell on November 2 to Gen. Richard Montgomery. Montreal was occupied 12 days later.

Both Israel Putnam (Top) and William Prescott (right) are credited with the order "Don't fire until you see the whites of their eyes" at Bunker (Breed's) Hill.

Howard Pyle's famous illustration (1898) of the second British charge on Breed's Hill. ▼

WILMINGTON SOCIETY OF FINE ARTS, DELAWARE ART CENTER

Meanwhile Washington proposed another plan—an attack on Quebec by way of the Kennebec River. The march by Col. Benedict Arnold was one of the major epics of the war. After suffering incredible hardships through rough terrain and unusually bad weather, Arnold arrived at the outskirts of Quebec on November 9 with only 600 of his 1,100 volunteers. Montgomery joined him from Montreal and together on the night of December 31, they attacked the walled city in a blinding snowstorm only to be repulsed in disaster. Montgomery was killed and Arnold wounded. The first year of the Revolution ended on an inglorious note.

Benedict Arnold, who led the epic march on Quebec, September-November 1775.

Fort Western, Augusta, Maine, from where Arnold launched his expedition.

The ruins of Crown Point, New York, about 12 miles north and an outpost of Fort Ticonderoga.

George Washington takes command of the Continental Army, June 1775, Engraving by Alonzo Chappel.

DIXON TICONEROGA PENCIL COLLECTION

Henry Knox, Washington's chief of artillery, hauled 59 of Fort Ticonderoga's guns 300 miles across the mountains and snows of New York and Massachusetts for the American siege of Boston. Painting by Tom Lovell. ▲

The Declaration of Independence

On June 7, 1776, Richard Henry Lee, Virginia delegate to the Continental Congress in Philadelphia, introduced a resolution "That these United Colonies are, and of right ought to be, free and independent states, that they are absolved from all allegiance to the British Crown, and that all political connection between them and the State of Great Britain is, and ought to be, totally dissolved."

There was no great clamor in the Congress for passing this resolution. Though a majority of the delegates had already voiced their favorable opinions on the subject of independence, there was some opposition from the more conservative members. Unanimity was most important, so a vote was put off until July. In the meantime a committee was appointed to draft the declaration—Thomas Jefferson of Virginia, John Adams of Massachusetts, Benjamin Franklin of Pennsylvania, Roger Sherman of Connecticut, and Robert Livingston of New York.

The document that was submitted to the Congress for adoption was for the most part the work of Jefferson. He had submitted his "rough draft" to the committee for comments and there were minor alterations made, but when the final copy was presented it was Jefferson placing "before mankind the common sense of the subject, in terms so firm and plain as to command their assent, and to justify ourselves in the independent stand we are compelled to take."

Historian Dumas Malone says "this most famous American political document belongs indisputably to Jefferson." The 33 year old Virginian had succeeded with eloquence in expressing the American mind.

The chamber in which the Declaration of Independence was adopted by the Congress July 4, 1776 in Philadelphia.

On July 2 the Congress adopted Lee's resolution and then on July 4 the formal Declaration of Independence was adopted. Contrary to popular belief the document was not signed by all members of the Congress on that day. Although independence was voted July 4, the completed signing was not accomplished until August 2 and not in an assembled body as depicted in John Trumbull's famous painting. It is of little consequence, however, since the American people, through their representatives in Congress, had pledged their "lives, fortunes, and sacred honor" to being free and inde-pendent; and had so given notice to Great Britain and the world.

John Adams wrote to his wife, Abigail: "it [July 4th] ought to be celebrated, as the day of deliverance, by solemn acts of devotion to God Almighty. It ought to be solemnized with pomp and parade, with shows, games, sports, guns, bells, bonfires, and illuminations, from one end of this continent to the other, from this time forward, evermore." And so it has been.

In CONGRESS, July 4, 1776.

The unanimous Declaration of the thirteen united States of America.

When in the course of human events, it becomes necessary for one people to dissolve the political bands which have connected them with another, and to assume among the powers of the earth, the separate and equal station to which the Laws of Nature and of Nature's God entitle them, a decent respect to the opinions of mankind requires that they should declare the causes which impel them to the separation.——We hold these truths to be self-evident, that all men are created equal, that they are endowed by their Creator with certain unalienable Rights, that among these are Life, Liberty and the pursuit of Happiness.——That to secure these rights, Governments are instituted among Men, deriving their just powers from the consent of the governed,——That whenever any Form of Government becomes destructive of these ends, it is the Right of the People to alter or to abolish it, and to institute new Government, laying its foundation on such principles and organizing its powers in such form, as to them shall seem most likely to effect their Safety and Happiness. Prudence, indeed, will dictate that Governments long established should not be changed for light and transient causes; and accordingly all experience hath shewn, that mankind are more disposed to suffer, while evils are sufferable, than to right themselves by abolishing the forms to which they are accustomed. But when a long train of abuses and usurpations, pursuing invariably the same Object evinces a design to reduce them under absolute Despotism, it is their right, it is their duty, to throw off such Government, and to provide new Guards for their future security.——Such has been the patient sufferance of these Colonies; and such is now the necessity which constrains them to alter their former Systems of Government. The history of the present King of Great Britain is a history of repeated injuries and usurpations, all having in direct object the establishment of an absolute Tyranny over these States. To prove this, let Facts be submitted to a candid world.

He has refused his Assent to Laws, the most wholesome and necessary for the public good.

He has forbidden his Governors to pass Laws of immediate and pressing importance, unless suspended in their operation till his Assent should be obtained; and when so suspended, he has utterly neglected to attend to them.

He has refused to pass other Laws for the accommodation of large districts of people, unless those people would relinquish the right of Representation in the Legislature, a right inestimable to them and formidable to tyrants only.

He has called together legislative bodies at places unusual, uncomfortable, and distant from the depository of their public Records, for the sole purpose of fatiguing them into compliance with his measures.

He has dissolved Representative Houses repeatedly, for opposing with manly firmness his invasions on the rights of the people.

He has refused for a long time, after such dissolutions, to cause others to be elected; whereby the Legislative powers, incapable of Annihilation, have returned to the People at large for their exercise; the State remaining in the mean time exposed to all the dangers of invasion from without, and convulsions within.

He has endeavoured to prevent the population of these States; for that purpose obstructing the Laws for Naturalization of Foreigners; refusing to pass others to encourage their migrations hither, and raising the conditions of new Appropriations of Lands.

He has obstructed the Administration of Justice, by refusing his Assent to Laws for establishing judiciary powers.

He has made Judges dependent on his Will alone, for the tenure of their offices, and the amount and payment of their salaries.

He has erected a multitude of New Offices, and sent hither swarms of Officers to harrass our people, and eat out their substance.

He has kept among us, in times of peace, Standing Armies without the Consent of our legislatures.

He has affected to render the Military independent of and superior to the Civil power.

He has combined with others to subject us to a jurisdiction foreign to our constitution, and unacknowledged by our laws; giving his Assent to their Acts of pretended Legislation:——For Quartering large bodies of armed troops among us:——For protecting them, by a mock Trial, from punishment for any Murders which they should commit on the Inhabitants of these States:——For cutting off our Trade with all parts of the world:——For imposing Taxes on us without our Consent:——For depriving us in many cases, of the benefits of Trial by Jury:——For transporting us beyond Seas to be tried for pretended offences:——For abolishing the free System of English Laws in a neighbouring Province, establishing therein an Arbitrary government, and enlarging its Boundaries so as to render it at once an example and fit instrument for introducing the same absolute rule into these Colonies:——For taking away our Charters, abolishing our most valuable Laws, and altering fundamentally the Forms of our Governments:——For suspending our own Legislatures, and declaring themselves invested with power to legislate for us in all cases whatsoever.

He has abdicated Government here, by declaring us out of his Protection and waging War against us.

He has plundered our seas, ravaged our Coasts, burnt our towns, and destroyed the lives of our people.

He is at this time transporting large Armies of foreign Mercenaries to compleat the works of death, desolation and tyranny, already begun with circumstances of Cruelty & perfidy scarcely paralleled in the most barbarous ages, and totally unworthy the Head of a civilized nation.

He has constrained our fellow Citizens taken Captive on the high Seas to bear Arms against their Country, to become the executioners of their friends and Brethren, or to fall themselves by their Hands.

He has excited domestic insurrections amongst us, and has endeavoured to bring on the inhabitants of our frontiers, the merciless Indian Savages, whose known rule of warfare, is an undistinguished destruction of all ages, sexes and conditions.

In every stage of these Oppressions We have Petitioned for Redress in the most humble terms: Our repeated Petitions have been answered only by repeated injury. A Prince, whose character is thus marked by every act which may define a Tyrant, is unfit to be the ruler of a free people.

Nor have We been wanting in attentions to our British brethren. We have warned them from time to time of attempts by their legislature to extend an unwarrantable jurisdiction over us. We have reminded them of the circumstances of our emigration and settlement here. We have appealed to their native justice and magnanimity, and we have conjured them by the ties of our common kindred to disavow these usurpations, which, would inevitably interrupt our connections and correspondence. They too have been deaf to the voice of justice and of consanguinity. We must, therefore, acquiesce in the necessity, which denounces our Separation, and hold them, as we hold the rest of mankind, Enemies in War, in Peace Friends.

We, therefore, the Representatives of the united States of America, in General Congress, Assembled, appealing to the Supreme Judge of the world for the rectitude of our intentions, do, in the Name, and by Authority of the good People of these Colonies, solemnly publish and declare, That these United Colonies are, and of Right ought to be Free and Independent States; that they are Absolved from all Allegiance to the British Crown, and that all political connection between them and the State of Great Britain, is and ought to be totally dissolved; and that as Free and Independent States, they have full Power to levy War, conclude Peace, contract Alliances, establish Commerce, and to do all other Acts and Things which Independent States may of right do.——And for the support of this Declaration, with a firm reliance on the Protection of Divine Providence, we mutually pledge to each other our Lives, our Fortunes and our sacred Honor.

NATIONAL ARCHIVES

1776

Thomas Jefferson by Rembrandt Peale. ▲

Independence Hall, Philadelphia. ▶

The Declaration of Independence appearing on the opposite page has been reduced from the original in order to fit this publication. ◀

"We Hold These truths to be self-evident, that all men are created equal . . ."

— THE DECLARATION OF INDEPENDENCE, 1776

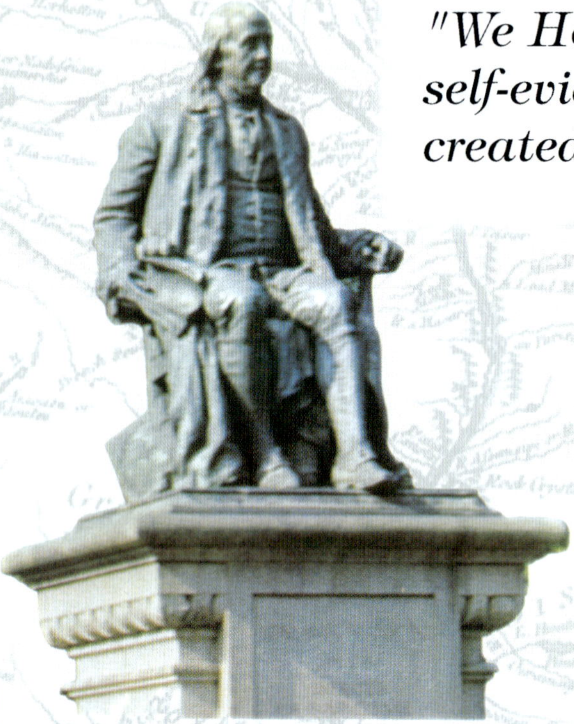

▲ *Benjamin Franklin, a member of the committee that drafted the Declaration of Independence; a bronze statue, by John Boyle at the University of Pennsylvania.*

ANDREW MELLON COLLECTION, NATIONAL GALLERY OF ART

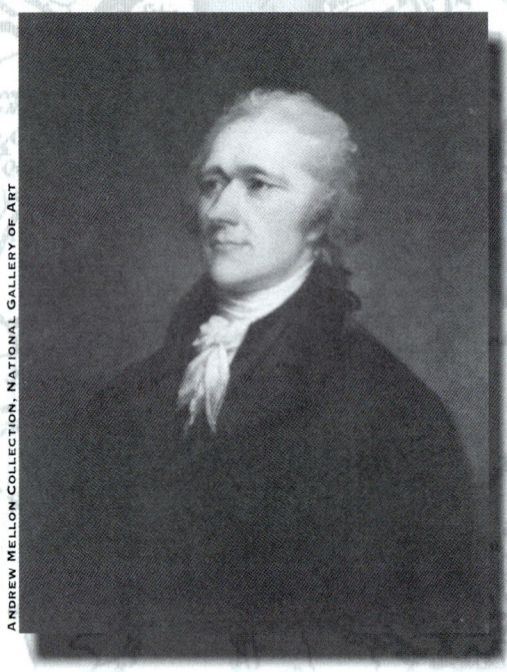

Alexander Hamilton, Continental Army officer, statesman, and first Secretary of the Treasury. Portrait by John Trumbull. ▲

The Signing of the Declaration of Independence, by John Trumbull. ▼

UNITED STATES CAPITOL HISTORIC SOCIETY, GEORGE F. MOBLEY, PHOTO., NATIONAL GEOGRAPHIC SOCIETY

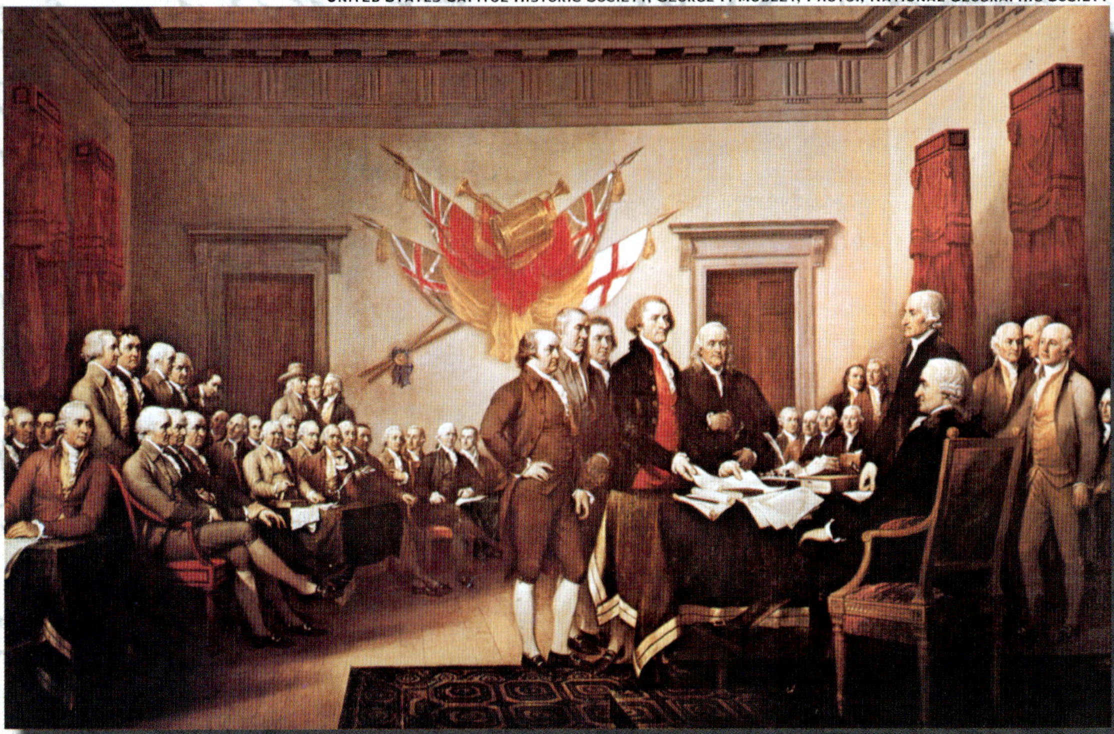

MASSACHUSETTS HISTORICAL SOCIETY

MASSACHUSETTS HISTORICAL SOCIETY

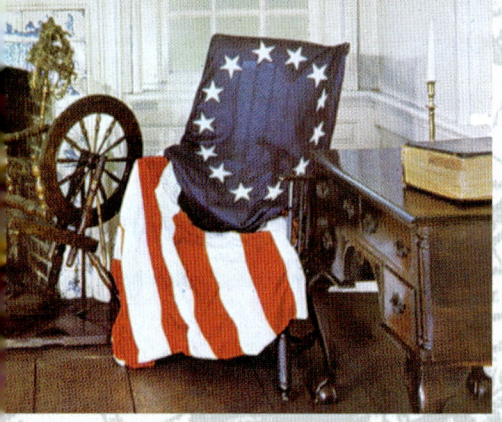

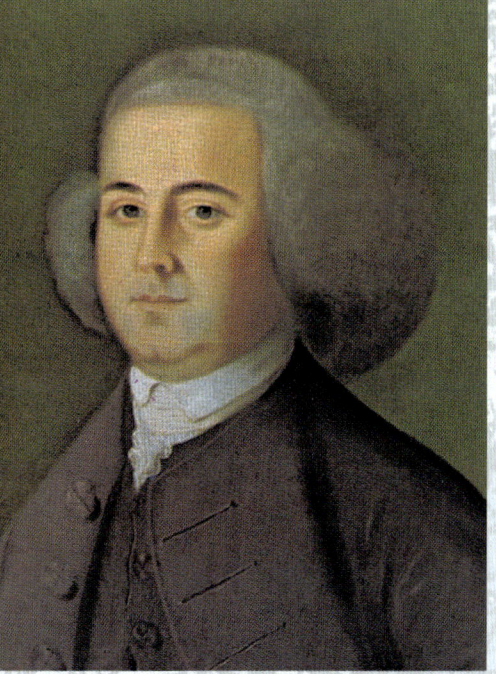

On March 17, 1776, Washington was credited with a major victory. The British evacuated Boston. Following heavy bombardment from guns brought over the snows from Fort Ticonderoga, Gen. Howe, who had replaced Gage as British commander, set sail from Boston with his troops. The Americans occupied the city immediately.

Fearing that Howe might land at New York City, the loss of which would be a serious setback for the colonies, Washington rushed troops to Manhattan Island. In late June about 30,000 British and Hessian mercenary troops were landed on Staten Island. Washington by this time occupied Brooklyn Heights. His army numbered 23,000. While he waited Howe's next move, Washington received a copy of the Declaration of Independence and had it read to his troops in the hope that "this important event will serve as a fresh incentive to every officer and soldier to act with fidelity and courage." The war had taken on a whole new meaning.

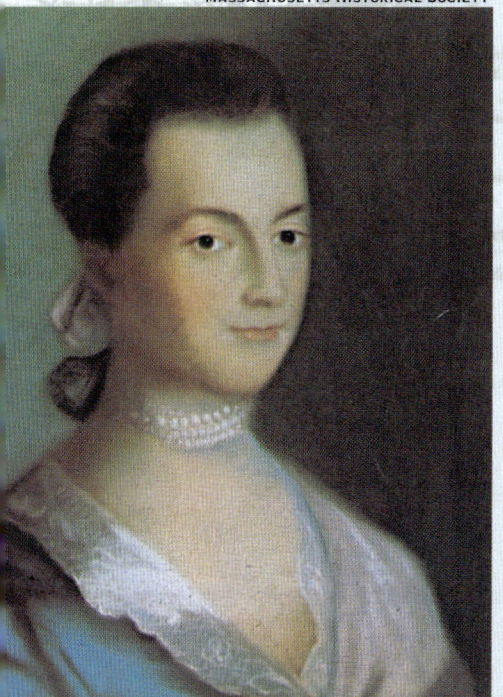

The Betsy Ross House, Philadelphia. There still rages a controversy over the flag Betsy Ross allegedly made for General Washington. (Top Left)

John Adams, Massachusetts signer of the Declaration of Independence, Vice President under Washington, and second President of the United States. Portrait by Benjamin Blythe. (Middle)

Abigail Adams, one of the better known Revolutionary women because of the published correspondence between her and her husband John. Portrait by Benjamin Blythe. (Lower Left)

This etching shows the arrival of British troops in New York City in September 1776 following the battle for Manhattan. ▲

> "I only regret that I have but one life to give for my country."
>
> — NATHAN HALE, SEPTEMBER 22, 1776

The British frigates Phoenix and Rose force the Hudson River passage between Forts Lee and Washington in the fall of 1776. Painting by Dominique Serres. ▼

On August 22, 1776, the British landed on Long Island and began a march around the American's advance positions. Early on the 27th British ships in the East River shelled the American rear as Howe attacked their front. By noon the rebels had fled to their fortifications with 200 killed and nearly 1,000 captured, including Gen. John Sullivan. Then Howe mysteriously settled down for a siege. Washington stayed until the night of August 29, when with incredible good luck he managed to evacuate 9,500 men with their equipment and supplies across the East River to Manhattan. He may well have saved the army from complete destruction and the country from total defeat.

The weeks ahead constituted a series of British advances and American withdrawals, until Washington at last crossed the Hudson River and retreated through New Jersey, across the Delaware near Trenton, and into Pennsylvania on December 7. Here he waited his fate. It was one of the lowest points in the

Emanuel Leutze's famous painting of Washington's crossing of the Delaware River on Christmas night, 1776. ▶

AMERICAN SWEDISH HISTORICAL MUSEUM

McKonkey Ferry House, Washington Crossing State Park, N.J. ▼

NEW JERSEY DEPARTMENT OF ENVIRONMENTAL PROTECTION

A small monument marks Washington debarkation point on the Delaware at Washington Crossing State Park, Pa. ▼

WASHINGTON CROSSING FOUNDATION

Revolution. "These are the times that try men's souls," wrote Thomas Paine. "The summer soldier and the sunshine patriot will, in this crisis, shrink from the service of their country; but he that stands it now deserves the love and thanks of man and woman."

The British halted their pursual in New Jersey. Washington had a respite, but he knew something had to be done to restore the confidence of the people and the morale of his army. Across the river at Trenton, Col. Johann Rail and 1,000 Hessians were celebrating Christmas. That night, December 25, 1776, Washington led 2,400 men across the ice-choked Delaware River, and early the next morning attacked the Hessians as they slept. Within an hour they surrendered. Washington had his first battle victory and an army in "high spirits."

While Washington struggled to keep his army together during the waning months of 1776, threats developed on other frontiers. On June 28 Adm. Sir Peter Parker launched a naval attack on Charleston, SC. Col. William Moultrie and 400 state militia successfully defended two island fortifications, one of which would later bear his name, against fire from 100 naval guns. It was a humiliating defeat for the British who had counted on heavy support from southern Loyalists. They pulled back and returned to New York.

"These are the times that try men's souls. . ."

— THOMAS PAINE, DECEMBER 1776

COMMON SENSE;

ADDRESSED TO THE

INHABITANTS

OF

AMERICA,

On the following interesting

SUBJECTS:

I. Of the Origin and Design of Government in general, with concise Remarks on the English Constitution.

II. Of Monarchy and Hereditary Succession.

III. Thoughts on the Present State of American Affairs.

IV. Of the present Ability of America, with some miscellaneous Reflections.

A NEW EDITION, with several Additions in the Body of the Work. To which is added, an APPENDIX; together with an Address to the People called QUAKERS.

N. B. The New Edition here given increases the Work upwards of One-Third

By THOMAS PAINE,

Secretary to the Committee for Foreign Affairs to Congress, during the American War, and Author of The Rights of Man, and a Letter to the Abbe Raynal.

LONDON

PRINTED FOR H. D. SYMONDS, PATER

1792.

[PRICE SIX-PENCE.]

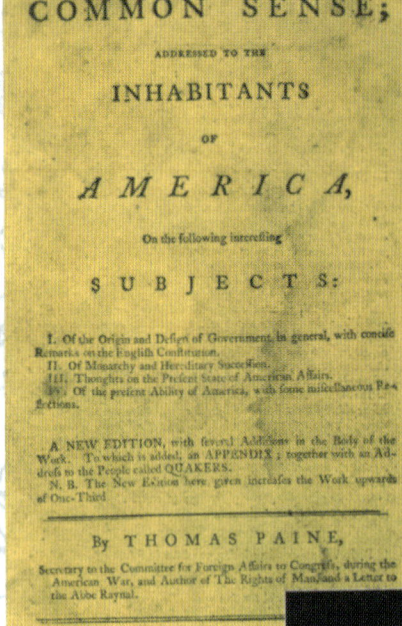

While the Americans were not so fortunate in another encounter with the British navy later that year, the Battle of Valcour Bay on Lake Champlain in October bought much needed time for the Continental Army and is generally credited as being a major turning point in the war. After forcing the Americans from Canada, Sir Guy Carleton, the British governor, set sail down the St. Lawrence for the Hudson River. At Valcour Island, opposite today's Plattsburgh, N.Y., his squadron of armed ships met Benedict Arnold's small make-shift navy of gunboats and inexperienced sailors. The Americans were almost totally destroyed but the delay caused Carleton to reconsider his timetable. It was not until the following year that the British again tried the northern route—this time to meet defeat at Saratoga.

NATIONAL GALLERY OF ART

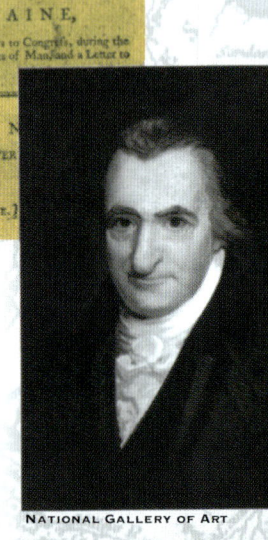

Thomas Paine, author of Common Sense, one of the most influential pamphlets published during the Revolutionary period. Portrait by John Wesley Jarvis. ➤

Adm. Sir Peter Parker's naval attack on Charleston, S.C., is repulsed by the American defense of Fort Moultrie. ➤

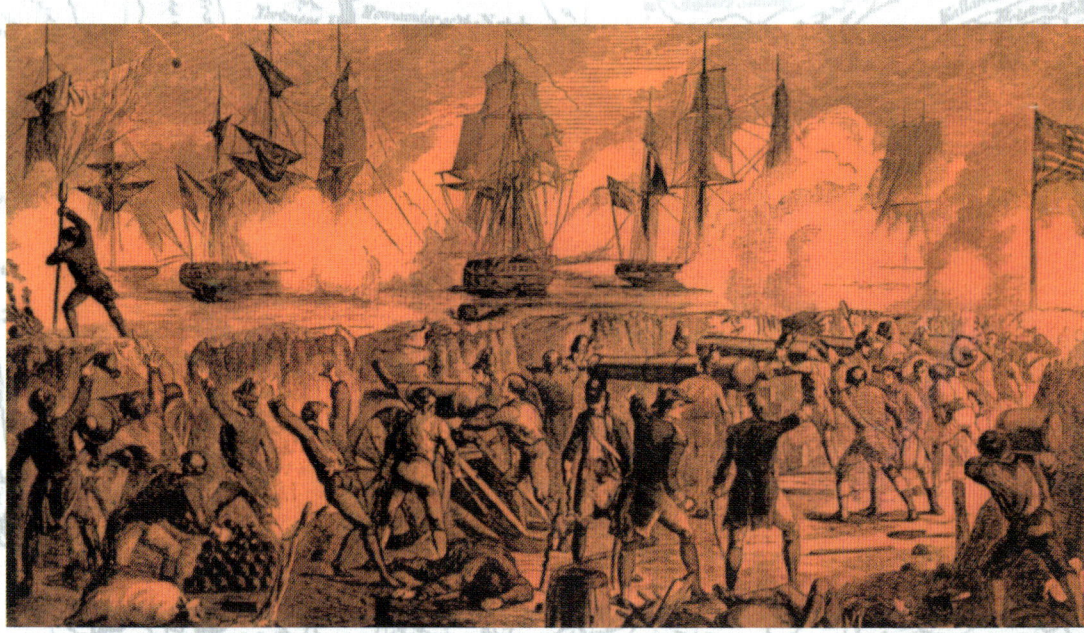

An aerial view showing the strategic location of Fort Ticonderoga on Lake Champlain. ▲

Mount Defiance on Lake Champlain from where the British directed fire on Fort Ticonderoga in 1777. ▼

The British were quick to react to Washington's success at Trenton. Cornwallis brought troops up on January 2 but instead of attacking immediately decided to "bag the fox" the following morning. That night Washington slipped around Cornwallis and successfully attacked British reinforcements at Princeton. Cornwallis fell back to Brunswick and Washington went into winter quarters at Morristown. The new year began on a victorious note.

Following page. Gen. George Washington reviews his ragged and hungry troops at the Valley Forge winter encampment, 1777-78. Painting by William L. Trego.
VALLEY FORGE HISTORICAL SOCIETY

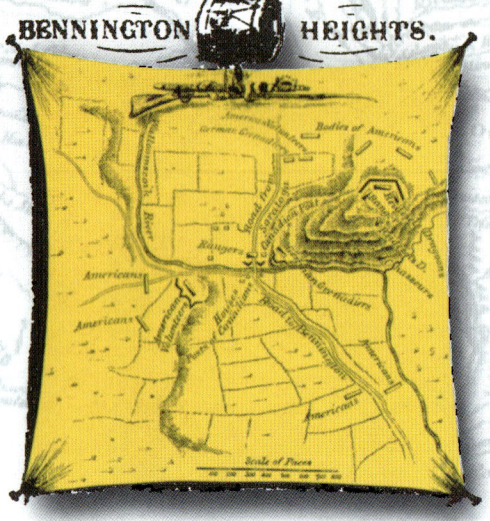

Benson J. Lossing's map of the battle of Bennington. ▲

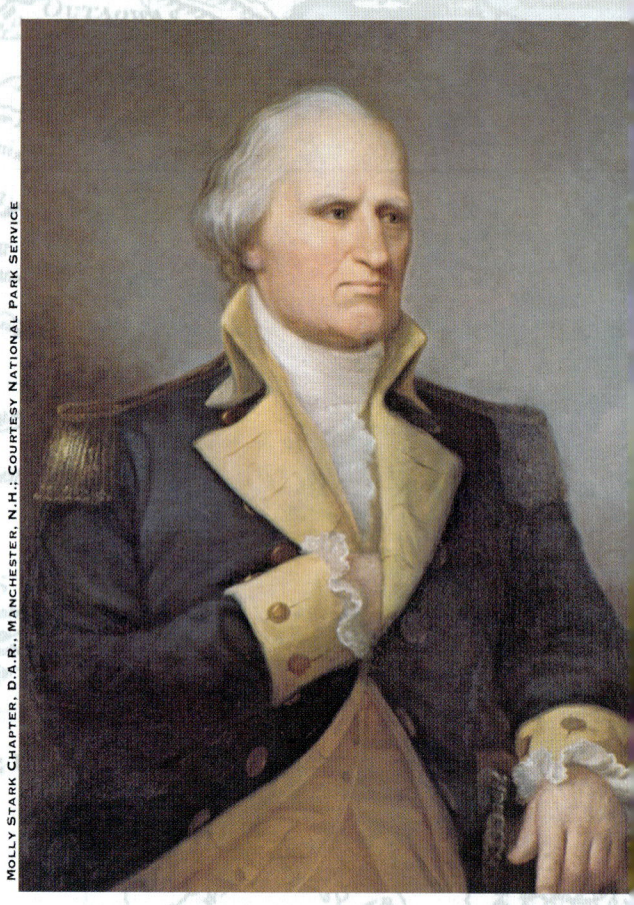

Gen. John Stark, hero of the Battle of Bennington. Portrait by U. D. Tenney. ➤

MOLLY STARK CHAPTER, D.A.R., MANCHESTER, N.H.; COURTESY NATIONAL PARK SERVICE

Raising the stars and stripes over Fort Stanwix, August 3, 1777. Painting by Edward Buyck. ▼

FORT STANWIX MUSEUM, ROME HISTORICAL SOCIETY

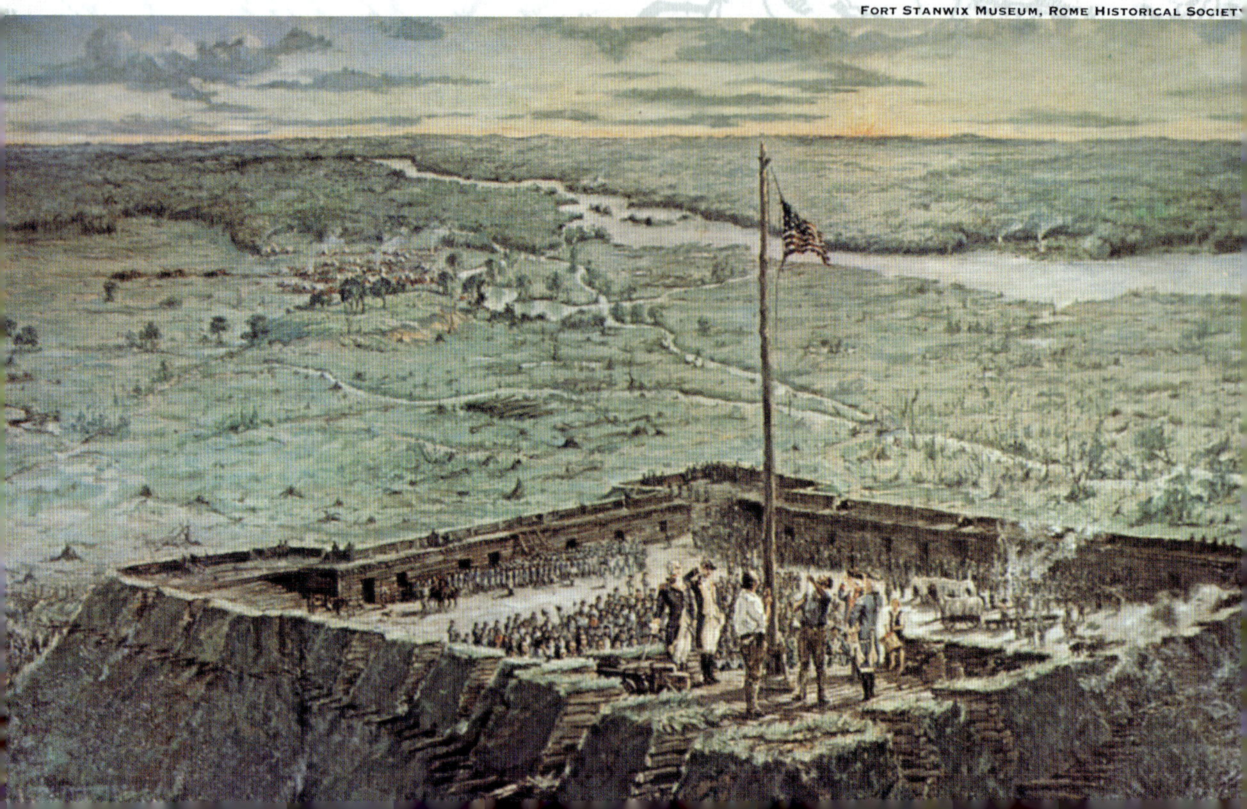

Fort Mifflin, Pennsylvania defense on the Delaware River. ◄

Burgoyne's surrender to Gates at Saratoga, October 17, 1777, from a lithograph in the Fort Ticonderoga Museum. (Bottom)

   By the spring of 1777 Washington's army was 10,000 strong but it was to see relatively little action. The main thrust of the British had shifted to the north in New York. The Lake Champlain-Hudson River invasion route was again considered. On June 17, Gen. John Burgoyne moved south from Canada with 10,000 troops with the understanding that he would be supported in his drive to divide the colonies with a sizeable force heading north from New York City. Fort Ticonderoga fell on July 6. Then things started going wrong. Attempts to take Fort Stanwix at Rome, NY, and a supply depot at Bennington, VT, failed with substantial losses. By this time it was obvious that there would be no troops from New York, yet Burgoyne pressed on.

   On September 13, Burgoyne ran into Gen. Horatio Gates' 9,000 Americans well positioned near the village of Stillwater, NY. On September 19 and again on October 7 Burgoyne tried to gain the upperhand. Both Battles of Saratoga ended in British defeat. On October 17 Burgoyne surrendered his army. Saratoga was a great moral victory for the Americans. When the news reached Europe, France recognized the American independence and pledged their assistance.

DELAWARE STATE ARCHIVES

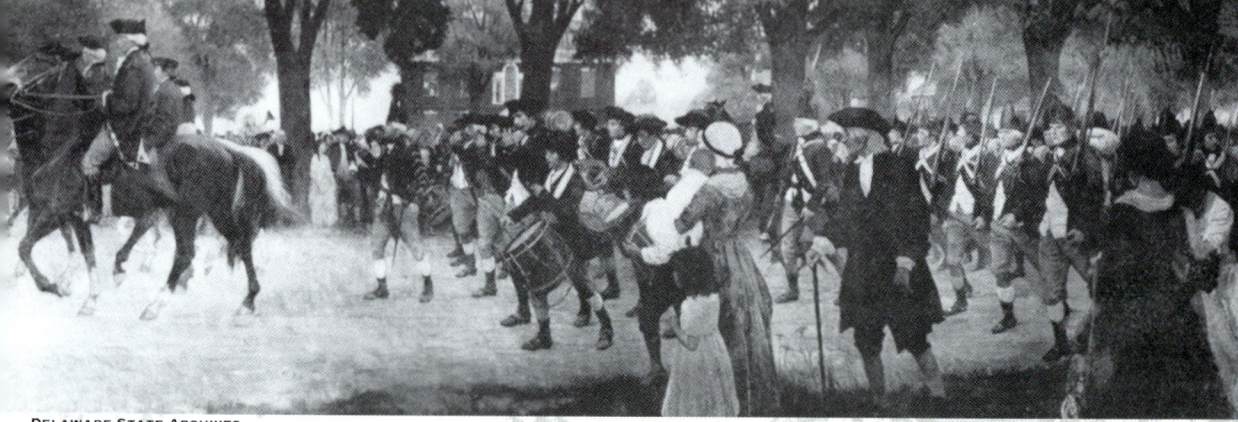

Delaware troops leaving the Dover Green, 1777. Painting by Stanley M. Arthurs. ▲

"Post two men behind each tree!"

— GENERAL NICHOLAS HERKIMER, AUGUST 1777

Meanwhile Washington's army was on the defensive again. Instead of going to Burgoyne's aid, Howe had headed for Philadelphia by way of the Chesapeake Bay. The two armies clashed at Brandywine Creek while the Continental Congress fled to first Lancaster and later York, PA. The British occupied Philadelphia on September 26.

A "surprise" attack on the British encampment at Germantown failed on October 4 and Washington was forced into winter encampment, this time at Valley Forge, one of the most tragic experiences of the Revolutionary years.

"Post two men behind each tree!" Frederick C. Yohn's famous painting of Gen. Nicholas Herkimer directing the Battle of Oriskany, August 6, 1777. ▼

UTICA PUBLIC LIBRARY

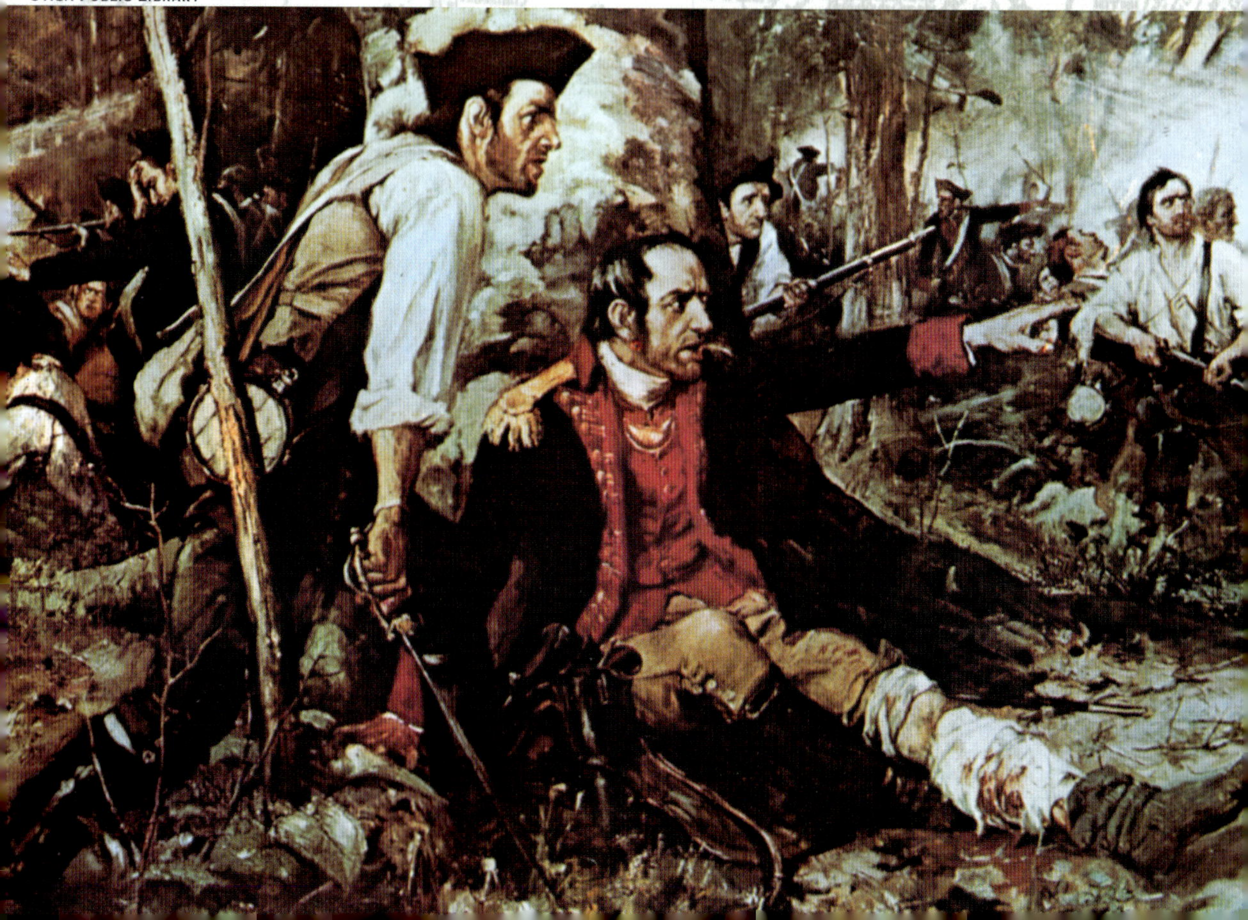

NATIONAL TRUST FOR HISTORIC PRESERVATION

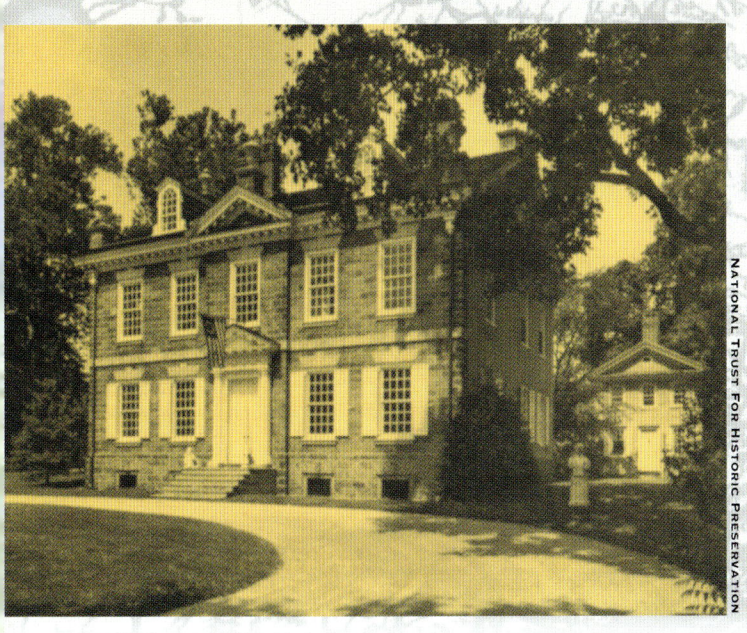

The Chew House (Clivedon) which featured prominently in the Battle of Germantown. ▲

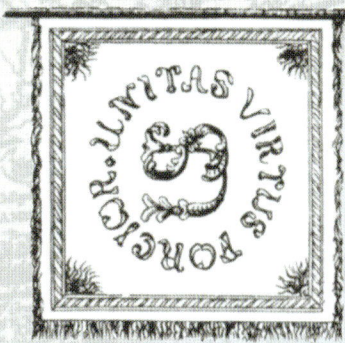

Flag of Pulaski's Legion, from a sketch by Benson J. Lossing; displayed at the Maryland Historical Society, Baltimore. ➤

Howard Pyle's famous painting of the Battle of Germantown. ▼

WILMINGTON SOCIETY OF FINE ARTS, DELAWARE ART CENTER

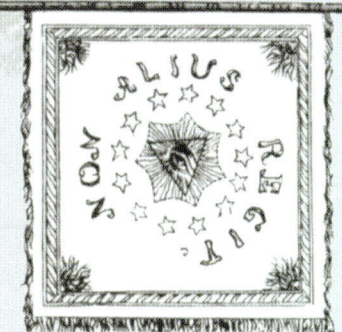

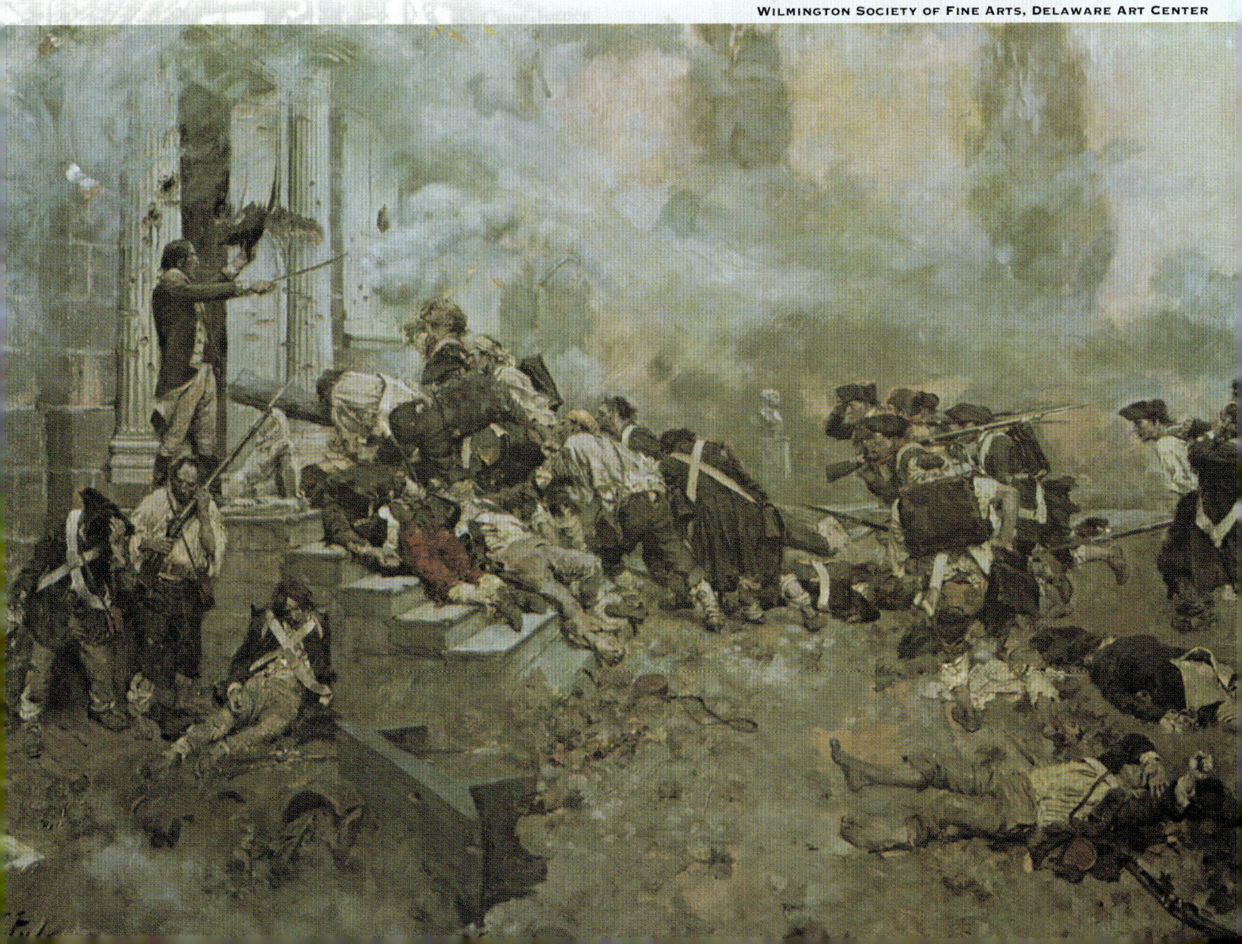

Valley Forge

"You might have tracked the army from White Marsh to Valley Forge by the blood of their feet"
— George Washington, Winter of 1777

"I am now convinced," the general wrote to Congress, "that unless some great and capital change suddenly takes place, this army must inevitably be reduced to one or other of these three things: starve, dissolve, or disperse in order to obtain subsistence in the best manner they can." Before the winter was over 2,500 had died and more than 2,000 deserted until the 11,000 were down to 6,000, nearly half of whom were unfit because of a lack of shoes and clothing. How the army survived can never be adequately explained—sheer determination and something called discipline and military spirit instilled by a Prussian officer, Baron Von Steuben, who drilled and marched the men beyond all physical endurance.

What came out of Valley Forge was something different—an army that was better prepared for the enemy, perhaps better than at any time in the war. Today Valley Forge has become a national shrine to the endurance of the Continental soldier. Forgotten is the fact that the suffering was due in great part to American mismanagement and to the indifference of a public still not convinced that armed rebellion was the way to oppose the Crown; Pennsylvania farmers sold their produce to the British in Philadelphia; British troops in New York City received New York grain.

Monument to New Jersey troops at Valley Forge. ▲

Baron von Steuben, Prussian officer and drillmaster of the Continental Army at Valley Forge. Painting by Charles Willson Peale. ▼

1778

Winter encampment, Living History demonstration at Morristown National Historical Park. ▲

Washington rallies his confused and disorganized men at the Battle of Monmouth, as painted by Emanuel Leutze in 1854. ▼

The early months of 1778 were good for the Continental Army. While it slowly recuperated from the winter the British command changed from Howe to Sir Henry Clinton, and with it came the evacuation of Philadelphia. As the enemy moved across New Jersey and back to New York, Washington left Valley Forge and followed. On June 28 Gen. Charles Lee struck the British at Monmouth Court House. The battle was so poorly executed that Washington took personal command, narrowly averting a disaster and beating back a British counterattack. Clinton moved on to New York, Gen. Lee was court-martialed, and the army went on to positions at White Plains, N.Y.

MONMOUTH COUNTY HISTORICAL ASSOCIATION

The War at Sea

"I have not yet begun to fight!"
— John Paul Jones, September 1779

All of the colonies, with the exception of New Hampshire, had an ocean coastline, or, in the case of Pennsylvania, a river that led to the Atlantic. Many had deep water ports and some had their own navy, but all had an abundance of mariners and these men were quick to take to the sea when the Revolution began. During the course of the war nearly 2,000 privateers harassed British shipping, capturing or destroying more than $18,000,000 worth of ships and goods. The word privateer means private man of war, and that is exactly what these were, privately owned vessels, commissioned by the Congress, out for a prize. While they had their successes, the romantic adventure of privateering drew heavily from the men and ships available for the official United States Navy.

John Paul Jones, By Charles Wilson Peale, 1781.

Sail and spar plan of 32-gun Frigate Raleigh launched March 21, 1776, at Portsmouth, captured off Penobscot September 27, 1778 by the British.

George Washington created the navy when he commissioned the Hannah on September 2, 1775 to check enemy supplies to Boston during the siege. Congress commissioned four warships one month later, and on November 25 the Continental Navy was established. Esek Hopkins was appointed Commander in Chief of eight vessels constructed at Philadelphia by the end of the year; the Alfred, Columbus, Andrea Doria, Cabot, Providence, Hornet, Wasp, and Fly. The little navy was put to sea on February 17, 1776, with John Paul Jones as the ranking lieutenant. Hopkins' only claim to fame with his fleet was the capture of Nassau, Bahamas, March 1776. Jones immediately established himself as the outstanding officer by capturing or sinking 22 enemy ships the rest of that year.

Some of America's naval battles were impressive but none had any significant impact on the war. There were Jones' raid on Whitehaven, England (he actually landed and raided a castle), and the spectacular but unimportant battle between his Bonhomme Richard and the British Serapis ("I have not yet begun to fight."); and there were other heroes such as Capt. James Nicholson of the Trumbull, and Capt. John Barry of the Alliance. For the most part, however, the Continental Navy did little more than form a foundation for the years to come when the United States would become a great sea power.

Although no American navy could challenge the British for control of the Atlantic seacoast, much less the ocean, the French could and late in the war did. DeGrasse and the French fleet off Yorktown in the Chesapeake Bay in October 1781, was the deciding factor in the British surrender.

John Paul Jones, after an adventurous career following the Revolution, died in Paris at the age of 45. Fifty three years after his death a movement was started to return his remains to America. In 1905 his body was found in the old St. Louis cemetery, almost perfectly preserved; so well preserved, in fact, that identification was relatively easy and acceptable to the American ambassador. On July 22, that year, the cruiser Brooklyn, escorted by four cruisers and seven battleships of the Atlantic Fleet, brought the body of America's most famous Commodore home. In 1913, amid great ceremony, as certainly he would have liked it, Jones was buried in a $75,000 crypt beneath the Naval Academy chapel at Annapolis. ◄

The first major naval action of the Revolution, and in many ways the most important, occured on Lake Champlain at Valcour Island on October 11, 1776. Benedict Arnold assembled 15 vessels, four captured and 11 constructed at Skenesborough, now Whitehall, N.Y. This makeshift, and totally inexperienced, American "navy" met the British fleet from Canada, 29 armed vessels and 24 other boats with men and supplies. It was probably one of the most valiant battles fought by any American force in the war.

Surviving that battle is the only intact naval vessel of the Revolutionary War, the gunboat Philadelphia. Today it is one of our most famous and certainly the largest of our Revolutionary relics, occupying an honored place in the Smithsonian Institution's Museum of History and Technology, Washington, D.C.

The Philadelphia was one of the first of Arnold's navy to go down at Valcour. Taking a British ball in its hull, it sank "about one hour after the engagement was over." For 159 years she rested almost totally intact in the cold clear waters of Lake Champlain just off Valcour Island. In 1935, Capt. L. F. Hagglund, diver extraordinaire, brought the Philadelphia to the surface, along with the ball

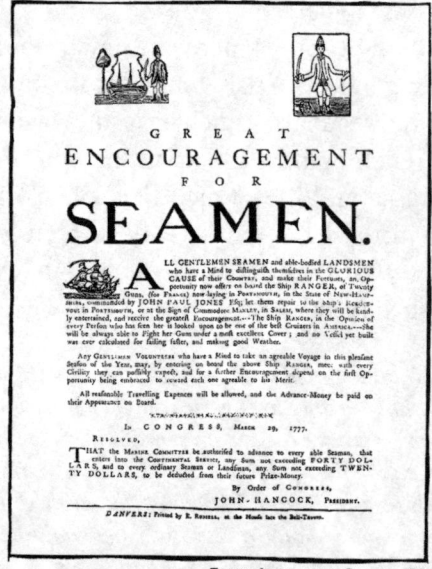

ESSEX INSTITUTE, SALEM, MA

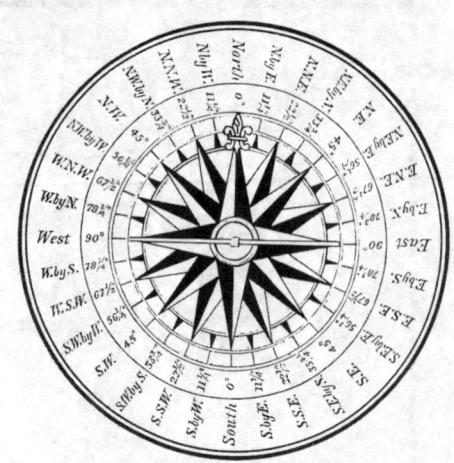

SHIPS OF THE CONTINENTAL NAVY
(some built, some purchased, some borrowed, some captured; numbers indicate guns)

Ship-of-the-line
America, 74.

Frigate
Serapis, 44, Indien (later South Carolina), 40, Bourbon, 36, Raleigh, 32, Hancock, 32, Warren, 32, Washington, 32, Randolph, 32, Deane (later Hague), 32, Alliance, 32, Confederacy, 32, Pallas, 32, Providence, 28, Trumbull, 28, Congress, 28, Virginia, 28, Effingham, 28, Boston, 24, Montgomery, 24, Delaware, 24.

Sloop-of-war
Ranger, 18, General Gates, 18, Saratoga, 18.

Ship (former merchantmen)
Bonhomme Richard, 42, Alfred, 24, Columbus, 20, Ariel, 20, Duc de Lauzun, 20.

Brig
Lexington, 16, Reprisal, 16, Andrea Doria, 14, Cabot, 14, Hampden, 14, Diligent, 12, Vengeance, 12.

Brigantine
Resistance, 10, Retaliation, (?).

Schooner
Racehorse, 12, Wasp, 8, Fly, 8, Pigot, 8.

Sloop
Providence, 12, Argo, 12, Hornet, 10, Independence, 10, Sachem, 10, Mosquito, 4.

Cutter
Cerf, 18, Revenge, 14, Dolphin, 10.

Lugger
Surprise, 10.

Xebec
Champion, 8, Repulse, 8.

A scale model of the gunboat Philadelphia exhibited at the Smithsonian Institution, Washington, D.C. ▲

A British fleet battles the French off Ushant in the painting by G. L. Ganne after Theodore Gudin. ▼

that sent her to the bottom. For many years Hagglund exhibited the gunboat around Lake Champlain. In 1961, she was brought to the Smithsonian, along with dozens of artifacts, including shoes, guns, shot, eating utensils, and uniform buttons, and is today a part of the Armed Forces Exhibit.

The rest of Arnold's navy was either destroyed in the battle or captured by the British and later lost. Pieces of some of these vessels do survive, however (recovered in various diving expeditions), and can be seen in such museums as the Naval Museum, Navy Yard, Washington, D.C.; Bixby Memorial Library, Vergennes, Vt.; Kent-Delord House, and the Clinton County Historical Society, Plattsburgh, N.Y.; Skenesborough Museum, Whitehall, N.Y.; Ancient and Honorable Artillery Company Museum, Faneuil Hall, Boston; and Fort Ticonderoga Museum, Ticonderoga, N.Y.

A reconstruction of Fort Harrod, a white settlement in what is now Kentucky, repeatedly attacked by British led Indians in 1777. (Top Left)

Clark leads his men across the Wabash River in the attempt to retake Fort Sackville. ▲

George Rogers Clark, from an original Portrait by John Wesley Jarvis. ◄

With the exception of raids on British forts and expeditions against Indians and Loyalists in New York and Pennsylvania, the war in the north was over. Again the action shifted to other parts of the country.

In May 1778, Col. George Rogers Clark commanded an expedition of 200 men against British forts in the Virginia claimed northwest territory, now Tennessee, Kentucky, Ohio, and Indiana. His first objective, Kaskaskia on the Mississippi, fell on July 5. With the help of the French in the region, and the advantage of the new alliance with France, Fort Sackville, at Vincennes, surrendered next. On December 17, Lt. Gov. Henry Hamilton in Detroit, recaptured Fort Sackville. Clark, at Kaskaskia, marched against Hamilton the following February and successfully regained Vincennes and effectually reduced British power in the northwest.

In the south, Savannah, GA, fell to the British on December 29, 1778. Augusta surrendered within the month.

Map of operations on the Delaware River. (Top Left)

Fifers and drummers of the Colonial Williamsburg Militia Company performing on Market Square Green, Williamsburg. ▲

Mary Ludwig Hayes, better known as "Molly Pitcher," comes to the assistance of her fallen husband at the Battle of Monmouth in this engraving. ◄

Mohawk War Chief Joseph Brant, who fought for the British and was responsible for much of the New York border warfare. Portrait by Charles Willson Peale. ▲

Fort Sackville is surrendered; from murals at George Rogers dark National Historical Park, Vincennes, Ind. ◄

Map of the siege of Savannah, October 9, 1779. ▶

1779

"Mad" Anthony Wayne, hero of Stony Point, attributed to James Sharpies. ▲

Gen. Benjamin Lincoln, commander of the Southern Department, 1778-79. Portrait by Charles Willson Peale. (Lower Right)

Ford Mansion, Washington's Headquarters during the Morristown encampments. ▼

America's greatest naval disaster occurred July and August, 1779, in the expedition under Capt. Dudley Saltonstall against British fortifications on the Penobscot River at Castine, Maine. In a badly managed amphibious operation, 500 Americans were killed or wounded and 39 of 41 ships were lost. Saltonstall was court-martialed. It was a dark day for the United States navy.

The Americans fared little better in the south. In the spring Washington sent Gen. Benjamin Lincoln with a detachment from the Continental Army to retake Augusta. His failure was compounded by an unsuccessful siege of Savannah from September 16 to October 18, where he suffered 800 casualties. The British victory gave encour-

Mrs. Benedict Arnold (Peggy Shippen) and child. She was judged innocent in the Arnold treason case until recent years when it was discovered she was involved. Portrait by Sir Thomas Lawrence. ▲

The 1715 Powder Magazine that played an important role in the Revolution at Willamsburg. (above right)

Castillo de San Marcos, St. Augustine, Florida, a British base for southern operations and a prison for American patriots. ▼

agement to Clinton to continue his quest for the southern colonies. On December 26 he sailed from New York for Charleston with 8,000 troops.

1779 was not without some redeeming value. Significant American victories at Stony Point on the Hudson with "Mad Anthony" Wayne, Paulus Hook, N.J., with Maj. Henry Lee, and at Newton (Elmira), N.Y., under Gen. John Sullivan, greatly bolstered morale.

Washington moved his army into winter quarters at Morristown in December. This would be the worse winter yet, as one historian has put it, making Valley Forge look like a picnic. Only the generosity of the local citizens saved the army from complete starvation.

1780

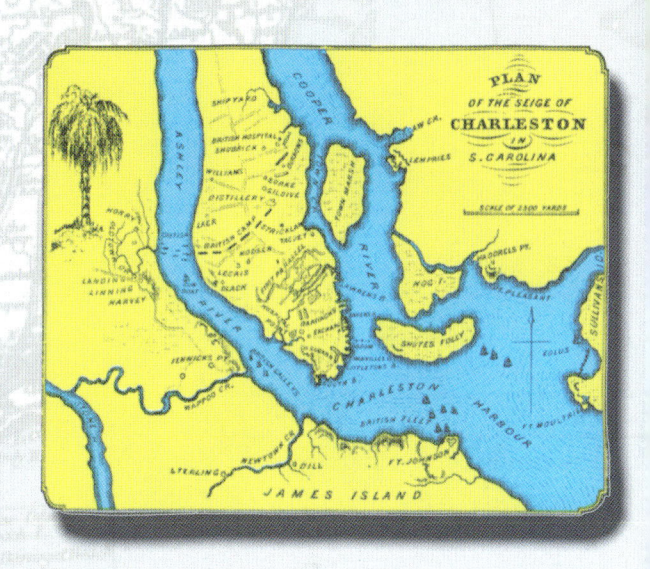

While the spring of 1780 brought relief to Washington's army, there was bad news from the south. The British arrived off Charleston in February and by April had the city surrounded. Within weeks Gen. Lincoln was forced to surrender his 5,000 troops, the largest loss suffered by the Americans in the war.

July brought new hope, however, as 5,000 French troops arrived at Newport, Rhode Island, under the Comte de Rochambeau. The strategy now was to confine the British to the south. To do this the Congress appointed Horatio Gates to head the southern department. Gates, with 4,000 men, confronted Lord Cornwallis at Camden, S.C., in August, and barely came away with half of his army.

The Gathering of the Mountain Men before the Battle of King's Mountain, by Lloyd Branson.

TENNESSEE STATE MUSEUM

Cannons at West Point overlooking the now peaceful Hudson River. ▲

UNITED STATES MILITARY ACADEMY

The American defeat opened the way for the British to move into North Carolina. Just as Maj. Patrick Ferguson, with 1,000 American Tories, or British sympathizers, reached the Carolina border, a band of 900 "mountain men" Patriots attacked. The Battle of Kings Mountain on October 7 was a major American victory, forcing Cornwallis to withdraw back to South Carolina and forever halting British influence in the Carolinas.

While an extraordinary Patriot courage was being exhibited in the south, one of the darkest chapters in American history was being written on the Hudson. On August 3, 1780, Gen. Benedict Arnold was placed in charge of the fortification at West Point. On September 23rd a British officer, Maj. John Andre, alias John Anderson, was captured, thus revealing Arnold's traitorous attempts to hand over the strategic location to the enemy for £20,000. Arnold fled to a British ship on the Hudson two days later. Andre was executed as a spy on October 2nd. Washington had lost one of his most valuable military minds.

Maj. John Andre, from a self portrait made in prison awaiting execution for involvement with Arnold's treason. ▼

1781

Not many miles from King's Mountain in South Carolina was a place called "Hannah's Cowpens" where cattle were grazed in the winter. Here on January 17, 1781, took place one of the most dramatic American victories in the south when Gen. Daniel Morgan defeated Col. Banastre Tarleton, one of the most feared men in the British army. Gen. Nathanael Greene, now commanding American forces immediately began enlarging his southern army. With 4,000 men, outnumbering Cornwallis two to one, Greene met the British on March 15 at Guilford Courthouse in a desperate fight that he almost won. Suffering 500 casualties, Cornwallis backed off to Wilmington, North Carolina, until April.

Conference Room at the Webb House, Wethersfield, Conn., where Washington and Rochambeau met to plan French participation in the Revolution.

"We fight, get beat, rise, and fight again."
— GENERAL NATHANAEL GREENE, 1780

The First Maryland Regiment charges the British Guard at the Battle of Guilford Courthouse.

Cornwallis's Surrender

"The play, sir, is over."
— MARQUIS DE LAFAYETTE,
OCTOBER 1781

While Greene went off to gain control of South Carolina, Cornwallis marched into Virginia where he was reinforced by Benedict Arnold, now commanding British troops. By summer Cornwallis had 7,000 men and was raiding throughout Virginia, no match for the Americans under Baron Von Steuben. And then on August 1 Cornwallis moved to Yorktown.

Gen. Charles Cornwallis, commander of British troops at Yorktown. ▲

John Trumbull's famous painting of the British surrender at Yorktown, October 19, 1781. ▼

UNITED STATES CAPITOL HISTORICAL SOCIETY, GEORGE F. MOBLEY, PHOTO., NATIONAL GEOGRAPHIC SOCIETY

Washington, meanwhile, had launched a series of coordinated movements with the French army and navy that resulted in a 21 day siege of Yorktown. Rochambeau marched south from Rhode Island and the French fleet under the Comte de Grasse blockaded the Chesapeake Bay. The last British route of escape was cut off. Cornwallis surrendered on October 19, 1781. Although there were other battles and the British did not evacuate New York until November 25, 1783, the American Revolution had come to a close at the little colonial village along the York River.

Lord Cornwallis was "sick" on the day his army was surrendered to the Americans. He sent Gen. Charles O'Hara to present his sword to General Washington. Washington refused to accept the surrender from other than the commander of British troops. Instead Gen. Benjamin Lincoln accepted for the Continental Army. John Trumbull depicted this scene in his famous painting.

Marquis de Lafayette, 20-year old Frenchman commissioned Major General in the Continental Army, July 1777. ▲

◀ *The living room of the Augustine Moore house was used for the British surrender discussions.*

The Hasbrouck House, Washington's Headquarters at Newburgh, New York, as seen by Benson J. Lossing in 1848. ▼

By the KING.

A PROCLAMATION,

Declaring the Cessation of Arms, as well by Sea as Land, agreed upon between His Majesty, the Most Christian King, the King of *Spain*, the States General of the *United Provinces*, and the United States of *America*, and enjoining the Observance thereof.

GEORGE R.

WHEREAS Provisional Articles were signed at *Paris*, on the Thirtieth Day of *November* last, between Our Commissioner for treating of Peace with the Commissioners of the United States of *America* and the Commissioners of the said States, to be inserted in and to constitute the Treaty of Peace proposed to be concluded between Us and the said United States, when Terms of Peace should be agreed upon between Us and His Most Christian Majesty: And whereas Preliminaries for restoring Peace between Us and His Most Christian Majesty were signed at *Versailles* on the Twentieth Day of *January* last, by the Ministers of Us and the Most Christian King: And whereas Preliminaries for restoring Peace between Us and the King of *Spain* were also signed at *Versailles* on the Twentieth Day of *January* last, between the Ministers of Us and the King of *Spain*: And whereas, for putting an End to the Calamity of War as soon and as far as may be possible, it hath been agreed between Us, His Most Christian Majesty, the King of *Spain*, the States General of the *United Provinces*, and the United States of *America*, as follows; that is to say,

That such Vessels and Effects as should be taken in the *Channel* and in the *North Seas*, after the Space of Twelve Days, to be computed from the Ratification of the said Preliminary Articles, should be restored on all Sides; That the Term should be One Month from the *Channel* and the *North Seas* as far as the *Canary Islands* inclusively, whether in the Ocean or in the *Mediterranean*; Two Months from the said *Canary Islands* as far as the Equinoctial Line or Equator; and lastly, Five Months in all other Parts of the World, without any Exception, or any other more particular Description of Time or Place.

And whereas the Ratifications of the said Preliminary Articles between Us and the Most Christian King, in due Form, were exchanged by the Ministers of Us and of the Most Christian King, on the Third Day of this instant *February*; and the Ratifications of the said Preliminary Articles between Us and the King of *Spain* were exchanged between the Ministers of Us and of the King of *Spain*, on the Ninth Day of this instant *February*; from which Days respectively the several Terms above-mentioned, of Twelve Days, of One Month, of Two Months, and of Five Months, are to be computed: And whereas it is Our Royal Will and Pleasure that the Cessation of Hostilities between Us and the States General of the *United Provinces*, and the United States of *America*, should be agreeable to the Epochs fixed between Us and the Most Christian King:

We have thought fit, by and with the Advice of Our Privy Council, to notify the same to all Our loving Subjects; and We do declare, that Our Royal Will and Pleasure is, and We do hereby strictly charge and command all Our Officers, both at Sea and Land, and all other Our Subjects whatsoever, to forbear all Acts of Hostility, either by Sea or Land, against His Most Christian Majesty, the King of *Spain*, the States General of the *United Provinces*, and the United States of *America*, their Vassals or Subjects, from and after the respective Times above-mentioned, and under the Penalty of incurring Our highest Displeasure.

Given at Our Court at *Saint James's*, the Fourteenth Day of *February*, in the Twenty-third Year of Our Reign, and in the Year of Our Lord One thousand seven hundred and eighty-three.

God save the King.

LONDON:
Printed by CHARLES EYRE and WILLIAM STRAHAN, Printers to the King's most Excellent Majesty. 1783.

The Articles of Peace

1782-1784

American delegates to the peace treaty signing in Paris, September 3, 1783; John Jay, John Adams, Benjamin Franklin, Henry Laurens, and Franklin's grandson William Temple Franklin who served as secretary. The British delegate refused to pose. Painting by Benjamin West.

In April 1782 Benjamin Franklin, John Adams, John Jay, and Henry Laurens began peace talks in Paris. The preliminary Articles of Peace were signed in November and the following April ratified by Congress. The final peace treaty was signed in Paris on September 3, 1783 and ratified by Congress on January 14, 1784.

George Washington embraces his devoted friend Henry Knox as the Commander in Chief takes leave of his officers, December 4, 1783, at Fraunces Tavern, New York City.

"To the memory of the man, first in war, first in peace and first in the hearts of his countrymen."

— GENERAL "LIGHT-HORSE HARRY" LEE, 1799

George Washington left New York on December 4, 1783, after saying farewell to his officers at Fraunces Tavern. It was a sad farewell, one in which few words were spoken. The general raised a glass of wine in toast and then with trembling hands and lips, and with tears in his eyes, embraced each of his colleagues. On December 23 he resigned his commission to the Continental Congress then meeting at Annapolis. "Having now finished the work assigned me," he told the delegates, "I retire from the great theatre of action; and bidding an affectionate farewell to this august body under whose orders I have so long acted, I here offer my commission, and take leave of all employments of public life." And then after nine years of service to his country, nine years filled with heartbreak and triumph, he returned to Mount Vernon. It was Christmas Eve.

Of his army, Washington wrote: "it will not be believed that such a force as Great Britain has employed for eight years in this country could be baffled in the plan of subjugating it, by numbers infinitely less, composed of men oftentimes half starved, always in rags, without pay, and experiencing every species of distress which human nature is capable of undergoing."

The American Revolution was over. A new nation was born.

Martha Washington, by Charles Willson Peale, 1776. ▲

Mount Vernon, where Washington lived out his last days and died in 1799. ▶

The Washington family portrait by Edward Savage. ▼

"Proclaim Liberty throughout the land unto all the inhabitants thereof."
— Leviticus, XXV, 10

"The Spirit of '76," by A.M. Willard